P9-CBC-106

NATURE RIDDLES

GUESS WHAT'S GROWING

A Photo Riddle Book

By Kelly Barnhill

CAPSTONE PRESS
a capstone imprint

A+ Books are published by Capstone Press,
151 Good Counsel Drive, P.O. Box 669, Mankato, Minnesota 56002.
www.capstonepress.com

092009
005620LKS10

Books published by Capstone Press are manufactured with paper containing at least 10 percent post-consumer waste.

Library of Congress Cataloging-in-Publication Data
Barnhill, Kelly Regan.
 Guess what's growing: a photo riddle book / by Kelly Barnhill.
 p. cm.
 Includes bibliographical references and index.
 Summary: "Photographs and simple text present how animals change as they grow up" — Provided by publisher.
 ISBN 978-1-4296-3918-7 (library binding)
 1. Morphology (Animals) — Juvenile literature. I. Title.
QL799.3.B37 2010
591.56 — dc22   2009040495

Credits

Jenny Marks, editor; Veronica Bianchini, designer; Svetlana Zhurkin, media researcher; Laura Manthe, production specialist

Photo Credits

Alamy/Stephen Frink Collection, 13
Creatas, 8, 22
Digital Vision, 28
Getty Images/National Geographic/George Grall, 19; Riser/John Lund, 15
iStockphoto/AVTG, 26; Steve Snyder, 17
Minden Pictures/Katherine Feng, 21; Mitsuaki Iwago, 27
Peter Arnold/Fritz Polking, 23
Photodisc, 12
Shutterstock/Craig Barhorst, 9; Dmitry Oshchepkov, 4 (inset); Doug Lemke, 18; Fouquin, 20; Four Oaks, 11; Kati Molin, 4–5; Monkey Business Images, 6–7; Neale Cousland, 24; Olya Telnova, 25; Sascha Burkard, cover; Studiotouch, 10; tubuceo, 14; Yuriy Brykaylo, 16
Svetlana Zhurkin, 29
Ted Barnhill, 32

Note to Parents, Teachers, and Librarians

Nature Riddles uses a nonfiction riddle format to introduce science concepts to young readers. Guess What's Growing is designed to be read aloud to a pre-reader, or to be read independently by an early reader. Deciphering word riddles and analyzing photos engages readers' critical thinking skills and heightens visual literacy. Nature Riddles promotes practice of the scientific inquiry process, through engaging children in observing, analyzing, guessing, and solving each science riddle.

In memory of Ashley, page 29. Rest in peace, little one.

TABLE OF CONTENTS

INTRODUCTION

Have you ever held a baby? Babies have soft, small bodies. Their heads flop from side to side. Their muscles aren't strong enough to hold them steady.

Does a baby stay that way forever? Do you look the same as when you were a baby?

Of course not! All babies grow and grow. Their little arms and legs stretch out. Their teeth grow out of their gums. Their muscles get stronger and stronger.

All living things change as they grow. Fawns lose their spots. Kittens open their eyes. Tiny seeds become towering, leafy trees.

CAN YOU GUESS ...

... WHAT'S GROWING IN EACH PICTURE?

HIDDEN HATCHLING

Three eggs as blue as the sky
quietly lie inside a nest.
But in each shell, a body forms.
It moves and wiggles and doesn't rest.
From gooey yolk new muscles grow
with legs, wings, and bright black eyes.
Soon a beak breaks open the shell.
The legs will stand. The wings will fly.

GUESS WHAT'S GROWING!

A ROBIN!

After two weeks in its egg, a baby robin is ready to come out. Sound easy? It isn't! To hatch out of its egg, the baby has to peck all day.

A SPOTTY SON

When I'm born I can't see or walk.
My mother holds me close.
She keeps me hidden from the group,
She watches as I doze.
I'm awkward when I start to grow.
I trip on my too-big paws.
But my tail and hair will lengthen,
and so will my teeth and claws!

GUESS WHO'S GROWING!

A LION!

The lion cub has no mane and no roar. As he grows, his mane will get long and thick. His voice becomes big and booming.

LUCKY ONES

We're tiny eggs now,
but someday we'll swim.
And we'll have stripes,
bright scales, and colorful fins.
Our hiding spot will carry a sting,
but, lucky us, we won't feel a thing!

GUESS WHO'S GROWING!

CLOWN FISH!

Clown fish are born by the hundreds. These colorful fish hide in anemones' stinging tentacles. A coat of slime keeps clown fish safe from the sting.

AIRBORNE

First wish, then blow,
then try to catch us
floating slowly
through the air.
And where we land,
we'll root and grow
green arms, green neck,
and yellow hair.

GUESS WHAT'S GROWING!

A DANDELION!

Dandelions need only a tiny breath of wind to spread their seeds far and wide. They grow quickly to decorate our yards, parks, and fields.

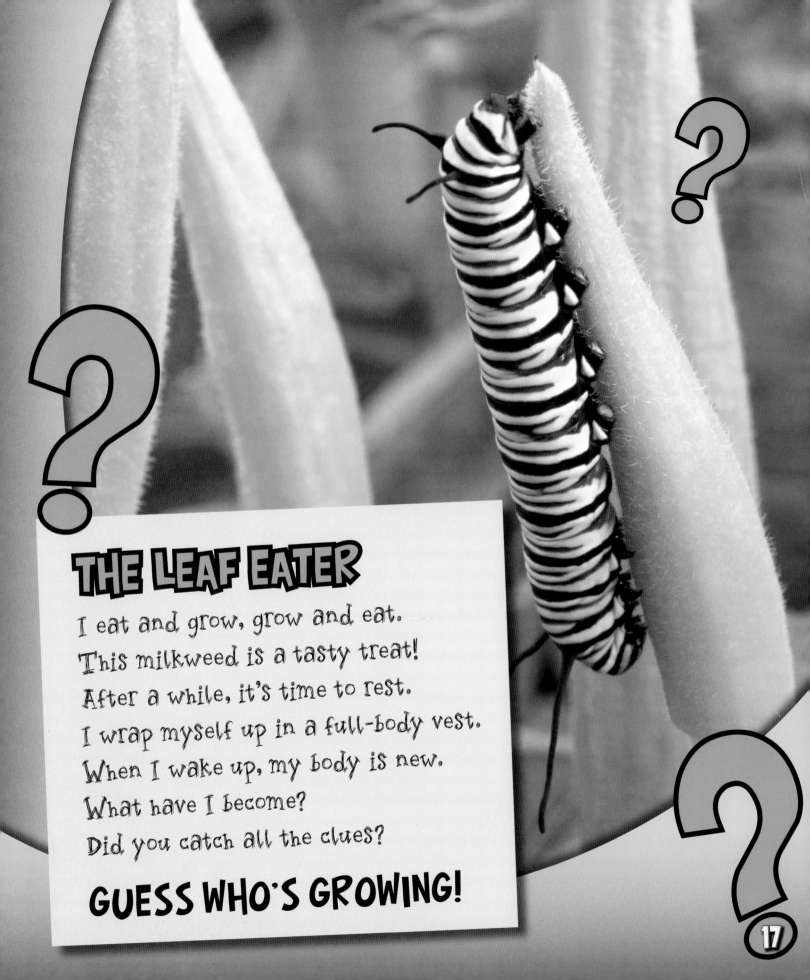

THE LEAF EATER

I eat and grow, grow and eat.
This milkweed is a tasty treat!
After a while, it's time to rest.
I wrap myself up in a full-body vest.
When I wake up, my body is new.
What have I become?
Did you catch all the clues?

GUESS WHO'S GROWING!

A BUTTERFLY!

Hungry caterpillars need lots of energy to form cocoons. Inside, their bodies change into beautiful butterflies. This process is called metamorphosis.

GOOEY AND GROWING

We don't have arms and don't have legs.
There's no shell on our eggs.
We're just little balls of goo.
Growing and forming is all we do.
But soon enough, we'll wiggle out.
Our sticky arms and legs will sprout,
and in the trees we'll leap about!

GUESS WHO'S GROWING!

A TREE FROG!

Red-eyed tree frogs lay gooey bunches of eggs on leaves above water. The eggs hang for five days, then hatch. The tiny tadpoles tumble out into the water below.

MUNCHING MUNCHKIN

I'm fuzzy and tiny, blind and pink,
no bigger than a lady's shoe.
But I'll grow and grow, both big and round,
by eating lots of green bamboo.

GUESS WHO'S GROWING!

A GIANT PANDA!

Tiny baby pandas need their mothers to survive. But these babies don't stay small forever. In a few short years, they go from 4 ounces (113 grams) to 250 pounds (113 kilograms).

WILD AND WOOLLY

I've never lived inside a nest —
I had a better place to rest.
I hatched upon my papa's feet
while mom was fishing in the sea.
My woolly down stays brown and thick
til I grow up — black, white, and slick.

GUESS WHO'S GROWING!

A KING PENGUIN!

King penguins have sleek, waterproof feathers, but their chicks are fuzzy and brown. Parents care for their chicks until the chicks' adult feathers grow out — about 14 to 16 months.

TINY GIANTS

Small and brown, a little nut,
I fell down to the ground.
With water and sun I'll root and branch —
I'll spread shade all around.

GUESS WHAT'S GROWING!

AN OAK TREE!

Although they are small, acorns have big plans! In time, tiny acorns grow into huge, shady oak trees. All they need is dirt, sun, and water.

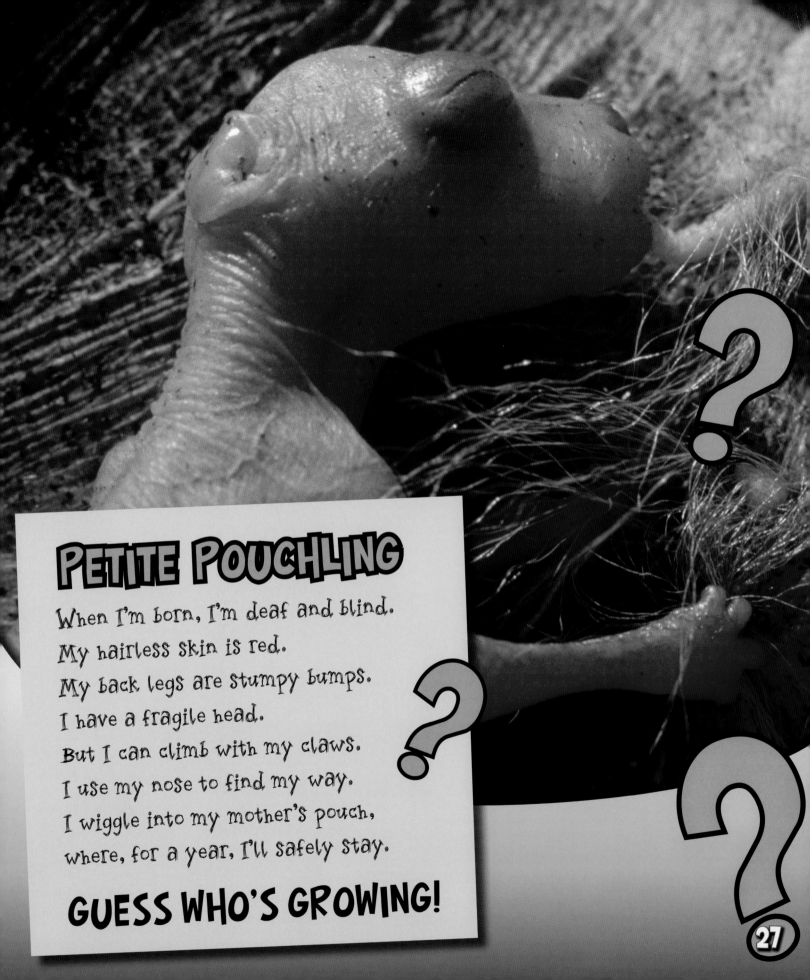

PETITE POUCHLING

When I'm born, I'm deaf and blind.
My hairless skin is red.
My back legs are stumpy bumps.
I have a fragile head.
But I can climb with my claws.
I use my nose to find my way.
I wiggle into my mother's pouch,
where, for a year, I'll safely stay.

GUESS WHO'S GROWING!

27

A KANGAROO!

A newborn kangaroo, or joey, is no bigger than a lima bean. Joeys do most of their growing inside their mothers' pouches.

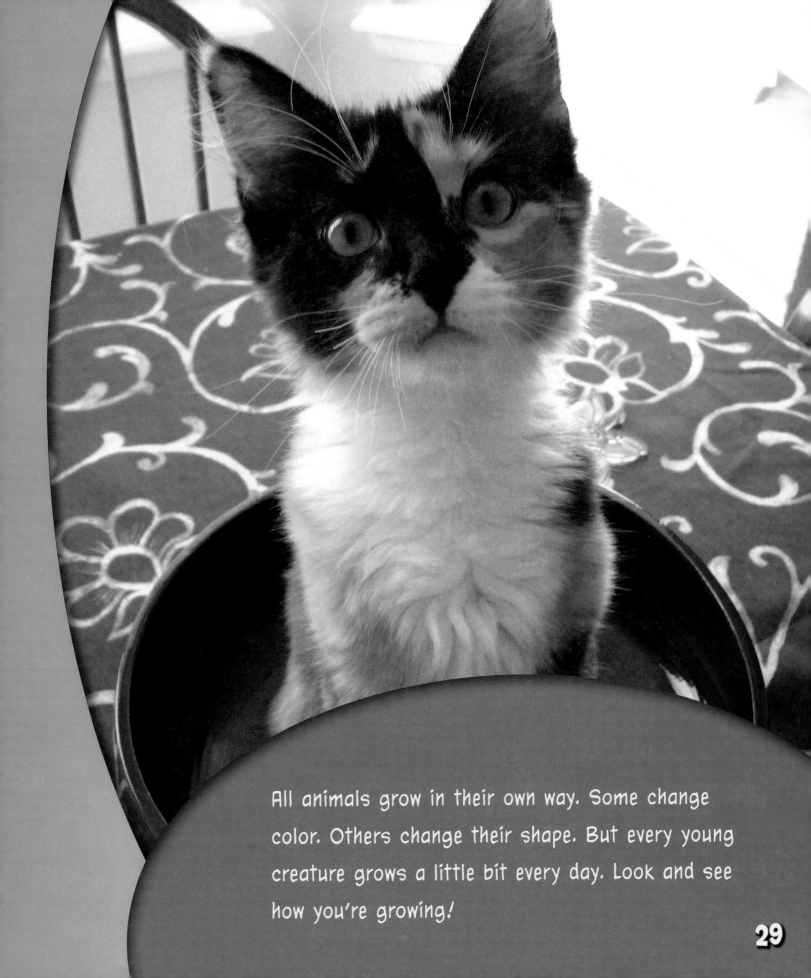

All animals grow in their own way. Some change color. Others change their shape. But every young creature grows a little bit every day. Look and see how you're growing!

GLOSSARY

anemone — an underwater creature with stinging tentacles

blind — unable to see

cocoon — a protective covering made of silky threads

deaf — unable to hear

down — the soft feathers of a young bird

fragile — delicate or easily broken

hatch — to break out of an egg

lengthen — to grow longer

metamorphosis — the series of changes some animals go through as they develop from eggs to adults

pouch — a small pocket of skin

READ MORE

Barnhill, Kelly. *Mystery Animal Tracks: A Photo Riddle Book.* Nature Riddles. Mankato, Minn.: Capstone Press, 2010.

Cooper, Jason. *Kitten to Tiger.* Animals Growing Up. Vero Beach, Fla.: Rourke, 2004.

Posada, Mia. *Guess What Is Growing Inside This Egg.* Minneapolis: Millbrook Press, 2007.

INTERNET SITES

FactHound offers a safe, fun way to find Internet sites related to this book. All of the sites on FactHound have been researched by our staff.

Here's all you do:

Visit *www.facthound.com*

FactHound will fetch the best sites for you!

INDEX

ABOUT THE AUTHOR

Kelly Barnhill has always enjoyed looking things up. When she was in third grade, she said that her two favorite series of books were Nancy Drew and World Book Encyclopedia. Now that she's a grown-up, she still uses her love of mystery and discovery in her writing. She's written about animals, monsters, hoaxes, fashion, fairies, schoolteachers, sewer systems, princesses, and other subjects too numerous to name. The best part of being a writer, she thinks, is that you always get to learn something new.